Journals and Logs

Men, women, and children throughout history have recorded their thoughts in journals.

- Lewis and Clark
- Thomas Edison
- Louisa May Alcott
- George Washington
- Christopher Columbus
- Beatrix Potter

Modern men, women, and children continue to record their ideas in logs and journals.

- Anne Frank,
  Nazi concentration camp victim
- Ambassador John Kenneth Galbraith,
  US Ambassador to India
- Jane Goodall,
  animal behaviorist
- Bruce Laingen,
  Iranian hostage

Today, teachers and students are using journals as they write to learn.

- Mrs. Jones
- Matthew
- Emily
- José

D1530609

An Introduction to Journals and Logs

What Are They?

In today's classrooms, teachers and students are using journals and logs daily. To the observer, a journal or log often looks like any student notebook. It is in the content that the value of journals and logs becomes clear. Students' notebooks of the past have been simply collections of others' thoughts—the thoughts and ideas of teachers, authors of books, speakers of the day. Today's journals and logs are:

- personal records of experiences,
- running accounts of work,
- tools that stimulate thought, and
- safe places for students to stretch and grow as learners.

Students use the journals and logs to:

- note their own observations,
- to imagine,
- to wonder,
- to worry, and
- to connect new information with things they already know.

The use of journals and logs as learning tools is based on the idea that students write to learn. Teachers who use them believe:

- Writing organizes and clarifies thoughts.
- Writing is one way students can think their way into a subject and make it their own.
- Writing enables learners to find out what they know and don't know about what they are trying to learn.

"Putting an idea in words is like defrosting a window. The idea is vague, out there in the murk, and it slowly gathers itself into sensible shape as it is written." [1]

Emergent writers can draw their ideas in journals, adding a word or two of explanation or having the teacher or cross-age tutor write the child's ideas next to the picture.

1. William Zinsser, Writing to Learn, (New York: Harper & Row, 1988), Page 16.

Why Should You Use Them?

Using logs and journals fosters learning in numerous ways:

- Students who use journals and logs are actively engaged in their own learning.
- Journals give students an opportunity to reflect on and clarify their thinking.
- Journal writing stimulates classroom discussion.
- Journal writing clarifies hazy issues and reinforces learning.
- Journal writing stimulates imaginations.
- Every journal entry is individualized.

When Should You Use Them?

Journals and logs should be used throughout the day, at different times, for different purposes, to "take snapshots" of students' thinking.

- Write in journals at the beginning of a class period so that students can articulate what they already know about a topic or question.

- Write in journals at the end of a class period to summarize what students have learned and to provide an opportunity to connect this new information with previous experiences.

- Write in journals at the middle of a class period to focus students on an important concept.

- Write in journals to solve a problem.

- Write in journals to respond to ideas and literature.

- Write in journals to monitor understanding and progress.

Some Important Things to Remember About Journals and Logs

1. Journal writing is meant to be shared. Dialogue journals are shared with one other person, but other types of journals and logs are often shared with classmates during discussions and are used a springboard for additional writing and learning.

2. Journal use is directly related to curricular study. Journal writing is interdisciplinary. It provides important bridges between different areas of the curriculum.

3. Journal entries are not finished products. They represent early states in a student's thinking.

4. Journal writing is not a one-time event. Its regular use makes it a valuable learning tool.

5. Students need instruction in both the content to be included and the procedures for writing in journals.

6. Journal writing should include choices. The choices might relate to topics, how the topic is approached, and the writing style.

7. Journals and logs require an investment of time and energy as students and teachers develop the habit of writing.

8. Teachers should keep journals too. This practice will validate the activity and help to model appropriate entries for students.

Different Kinds of Journals and Logs

This book presents the five variations of journals and logs described below. Teacher information and reproducible forms begin on the pages listed. Adapt these suggestions to fit the needs of your classroom and curriculum. Feel free to use an idea from the learning log section in your reading response journal.

Reading Response Journals (Page 10)

Sometimes called Literature Response Journals or simply Response Journals, these journals are used to capture students' reactions to books and to track their reading. The entries are varied and might include questions, comparisons, notes about highlights, evaluations, letters to characters, lists of character traits, predictions, and comments on style or mood.

Writers' Logs (Page 20)

A Writer's Log is a place to store ideas, feelings, memories, sensations, reflections, imaginings, and words. Experiences recorded in a writer's log are easy to retrieve and become the answer to "What can I write about today?"

Learning Logs (Page 32)

Learning Logs summarize learning and how a student feels about it. They are often limited to a particular subject (for example, My Science Learning Log). Entries include observations, questions, lists, and comparisons. They may take the form of words, graphs or charts, and even pictures. These logs help students to become aware of their personal learning processes.

Dialogue Journals (Page 44)

Dialogue Journals are conversations in writing. Most often the conversation is between the student and the teacher, but dialogue journals could be between cross-age buddies or student-mentor pairs as well. These journals are interactive — the two conversation partners comment on one another's entries. These written conversations encourage students to express themselves in thoughtful, informal ways and give teachers important insight into their students.

Field Notebooks (Page 50)

Field Notebooks are records of the observations, reactions, and questions taken from outside of the classroom. Primarily used in science and social studies, these notebooks provide data for classroom study.

1. Decide what type of journal or log you want to use in your classroom (page 5). Think about the purpose of the journal and how you will use it.

   Are you going to begin with a journal that records responses to a single unit in a specific part of the curriculum?

   Are you going to begin a writing log that will become a resource for future writing?

   Are you going to communicate through a dialogue journal with each student in your classroom?

2. Prepare the materials.

   Your students' logs or journals may be looseleaf notebooks or folders or they may be computer files. Whatever form they take, the individual pages should be connected or contained in some way so that they are not misplaced or lost over time. Assign a place for storing the journals.

3. Help students to see the value of keeping journals and logs.

   If possible, read from actual journals of famous people such as Lewis and Clark, Beatrix Potter, Thomas Edison, or George Washington.

4. Model initial entries.

You will need to model possible responses the first several times your students make journal entries <u>and</u> each time you introduce a new type of response. (See example on right.)

- Discuss the information that students are to respond to.
- Using an overhead or a classroom chart, set up a format for the response.
- Work together to write a sample response.
- Begin another open-ended response.
- Have students write in their individual response logs. Students can copy the class response or write one of their own, and then finish the open-ended response.

Example of how to model a journal entry:
    The class is reading *The Thirteen Clocks*. After reading Chapter 4, talk about the relationship between the Prince and Princess Saralinda.

Prompt:
How did Princess Saralinda feel about the Prince?

Sample Response:
Princess Saralinda wants the Prince to succeed. She is afraid that she will be frozen with the Duke forever. She can only say "I wish him well" because of a witch's spell, but her eyes look into his and speak a silent language. She throws him a rose in the darkness as he begins his journey. The rose tells the Prince that she loves him and waits for his return.

Prompt:
How did the Prince feel about Saralinda?

Open-ended Response:
When the Prince left the castle, he looked up at a lighted window and saw the Princess Saralinda standing there. He thought...

5. Schedule time for regular journal use.

The value of your journals will be increased if you integrate them into your everyday expectations. Journal writing works because every entry is an individualized assignment. Individual students are all engaged in the act of writing. This writing, even for a few minutes, forces individuals to generate ideas, observations, and emotions. Journal writing demands active learning. It's hard to daydream, doze off, or fidget while one writes.

6. After using the journals for a period of time, elicit student responses about the use of the journal and evaluate the journals' value to you.

As both you and your students recognize the value of journal writing, the process will become even more valuable. Use the journal as a reference file to help you monitor individual development and progress. Help students use their journal entries to develop the awareness of, and eventually, the commitment to, their own learning processes.

Evaluating Journals and Logs

Since writing in journals and logs represents part of a process, entries should not be evaluated as finished products. Journal writing is a step to completion of a project. The evaluation of journals and logs should emphasize the content.

- Students receive credit for participation.
- Journals are reviewed for patterns of good thinking or non-completion.
- Journals are used as a resource as in "open-journal testing."

While each journal is unique, good journals share these characteristics. They include:

- personal observations
- questions
- speculations and predictions
- evidence of developing self-awareness
- connections between personal experience and new information

The form below can be used for periodic evaluation of student journal use. It would be a valuable portfolio entry. Transfer individual student records to the ongoing class checklist on page 9.

- -

Name	Date

The entries in this journal include:

☐ personal observations   ☐ evidence of developing self-awareness

☐ questions   ☐ connections between new information and previous experiences

☐ speculations and predictions   ☐ regular, thoughtful journaling

Student comments:	Teacher comments:

Journals and Logs

Name	shows significant effort	personal observations recorded	serious thought evident	includes questions	makes predictions	connects information & personal experiences	demonstrates developing self-awareness

Reading Response Journals

Pages 13-19 are reproducible forms for use with your reading response journals. Reproduce them for individual students, use them to make transparencies for use with the overhead projector, or scan them to use with your computer.

Suggestions for using each page are given below. The suggestions are not meant to be inclusive. Use them as a springboard for developing additional ideas for responses.

Page 13 - Reading Response Journal Cover

Page 14 - Double Entry Journal Page

A double entry page requires that the student reflect and react to an entry that they have made. Often the left side is used before the reading is done, and the right side is used after reading is completed. Some examples of a variety of prompts and "student" responses are given below.

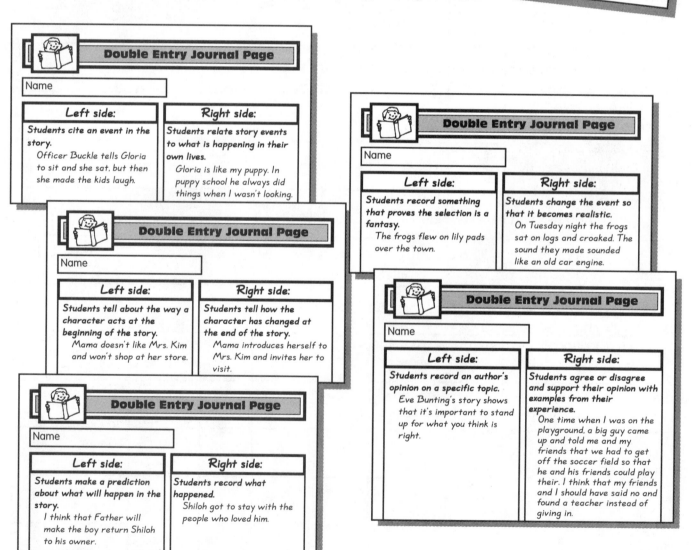

Double Entry Journal Page

Name

Left side:	Right side:
Students cite an event in the story.	Students relate story events to what is happening in their own lives.
Officer Buckle tells Gloria to sit and she sat, but then she made the kids laugh.	Gloria is like my puppy. In puppy school he always did things when I wasn't looking.

Double Entry Journal Page

Name

Left side:	Right side:
Students record something that proves the selection is a fantasy.	Students change the event so that it becomes realistic.
The frogs flew on lily pads over the town.	On Tuesday night the frogs sat on logs and croaked. The sound they made sounded like an old car engine.

Double Entry Journal Page

Name

Left side:	Right side:
Students tell about the way a character acts at the beginning of the story.	Students tell how the character has changed at the end of the story.
Mama doesn't like Mrs. Kim and won't shop at her store.	Mama introduces herself to Mrs. Kim and invites her to visit.

Double Entry Journal Page

Name

Left side:	Right side:
Students record an author's opinion on a specific topic.	Students agree or disagree and support their opinion with examples from their experience.
Eve Bunting's story shows that it's important to stand up for what you think is right.	One time when I was on the playground, a big guy came up and told me and my friends that we had to get off the soccer field so that he and his friends could play their. I think that my friends and I should have said no and found a teacher instead of giving in.

Double Entry Journal Page

Name

Left side:	Right side:
Students make a prediction about what will happen in the story.	Students record what happened.
I think that Father will make the boy return Shiloh to his owner.	Shiloh got to stay with the people who loved him.

Page 15 - Getting to Know a Character

Characters in stories are revealed by what they do, what they say, and what they think. The reader learns about them from the narrator and by what other characters say about them. This journal page helps students understand how authors develop characters. You may want to reproduce multiple pages so that students write only one entry for each question per page.

1. Have students fill in the chart as they review a story they have just read.
2. Then ask students to use their chart entries as they discuss the books they have read. Observe whether certain approaches to developing characters are used more than others.
3. Extend the experience by asking students to read another book by the same author and fill out a new chart about its main character. Does the author rely on the same techniques in the second book? Are the characters similar? What are the differences?

Page 16 - Comparing Two Stories

This journal page will help students to discover patterns in variations of the same story or in an entire genre of literature, such as folk tales.

1. Read two variations of a story. ("The Three Little Pigs" has some wonderful variations.)
2. Work together to fill in a chart like the one on sample page 16. Discuss the similarities and differences between the two stories.
3. Have students read a third version and fill out the chart as they read.
4. Extend this experience by using the same chart to compare two dissimilar stories. Try *Mirette on the High Wire* by Emily Arnold McCully (G.P. Putnam's Sons, 1992) and *Now One Foot, Now the Other* by Tomie de Paola (G.P. Putnam's Sons, 1981). Help students to discover common threads and themes.

Page 17 - A Letter to a Character

This journal page is a letter form. Use it to have students write letters to the characters in a story or novel. Or, have them write to an author and comment on the author's writing or characterization.

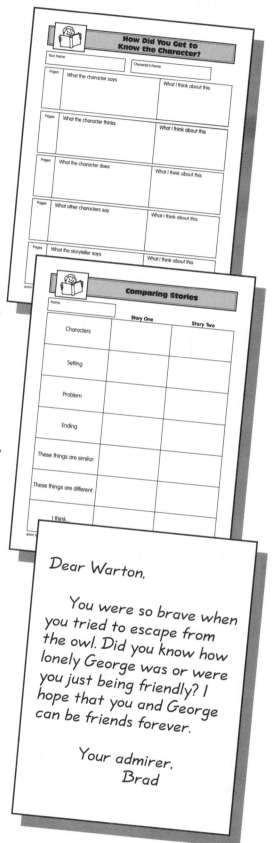

Dear Warton,

You were so brave when you tried to escape from the owl. Did you know how lonely George was or were you just being friendly? I hope that you and George can be friends forever.

Your admirer,
Brad

Page 18 - A Reading Log

Students may want to track their reading by maintaining a reading log. This journal page is designed to help students discover their personal reading preferences as well as simply listing the books they have read. When completed, this graphic summary is valuable to both teacher and student.

Page 19 - Mapping a Story

This journal page provides a convenient place for students to take notes as they are reading. They record characters, setting, conflicts, problems, figurative language, interesting phrases. When they are completed, use the maps to analyze the story and as a springboard for writing.

Note: Even emergent readers can use this mapping technique. Adjust the categories to fit their needs — a box for each character, a box for the problem, a box for the setting, a box for the solution. Allow them to draw and write their answers, adding the detail they gain by listening and reading.

Page 20 - What Happens Next?

Planning a sequel helps students to analyze the setting, characters, mood, and style of a story. They begin by identifying those elements in the original piece and then determining what they will be for the new piece. This log page helps students to organize this thinking. Have them take notes as they read the original story and then fill in the second column as they plan their sequel.

My Reading Response Journal

Name

Double Entry Journal Page

Name

How Did You Get to Know the Character?

Your Name	Character's Name

Pages	What the character says	What I think about this

Pages	What the character thinks	What I think about this

Pages	What the character does	What I think about this

Pages	What other characters say	What I think about this

Pages	What the storyteller says	What I think about this

Comparing Stories

Name

	Story One	Story Two
Characters		
Setting		
Problem		
Ending		
These things are similar:		
These things are different:		
I think...		

A Letter for You

Name

Date _____

Dear _____ ,

_____

_____

_____

_____

_____

_____

_____

_____

_____ ,

_____

My Reading Log

Name

	Book Titles						
Fiction							
Non-fiction							
Funny							
Exciting							
Scary							
Sad							
Animals							
People							
In the past							
In the present							
In the future							
Opinions:							
a favorite							
worth reading							
just o.k.							
didn't finish							

Mapping a Story

Name

Story title	Setting
.... Author	
Main character	Another main character
Problem	What happens
Words and phrases I like	How it ends

What Happens Next?

Name

	Title of Sequel	Title of Story or Book
When and where does the story take place?		
Who is the story about?		
What happens?		
How do the characters feel?		
How does it end?		

How to Use Journals and Logs EMC 577

Writers' Log

The Writer's Log is a resource for writing. It will include lists, story ideas, phrases, ideas, observations, and thoughts that can be used in later writing. Pages 23-31 are reproducible forms for use with your writers' logs. Reproduce them for individual students, use them to make transparencies for use with an overhead projector, or scan them to use with your computer.

Suggestions for using each form are given below. The suggestions are not meant to be inclusive. Use them as a springboard for developing additional ideas for responses.

You might also include these open-ended pages in your class' writers' logs:

- Story Ideas
- Things I See
- Notes to Myself

Page 23 - Writer's Log Cover

Page 24 - Words That Make You Feel...
This form provides a place to list words that make a reader feel a certain way. Begin with the categories suggested–frightened, angry, warm, loved, hungry, in a hurry–and then encourage students to add additional lists in categories of their own.

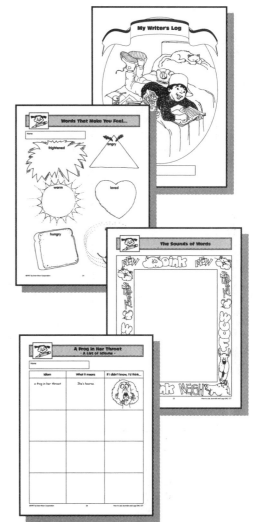

Page 25 - The Sounds of Words
Part of the magic of words is their sounds. Use this page to collect words that are fun to say and to listen to. The words may be onomatopoeic — they may imitate sounds — or they may just include wonderful combinations of sounds.

sassafras	whisper
galoshes	buzz
whoosh	blithely
marshmallow	zing
bamboozle	murmur
eucalyptus	splash

Page 26 - A Frog in Her Throat — A List of Idioms
An idiom is an expression that has a meaning of its own. When a lady has a frog in her throat, she is hoarse. The meaning of the idiom cannot be derived from the individual meanings of the words in it. Have students begin a list of idioms. As they listen for them they will become more aware of how often they use them in their own speech and writing.

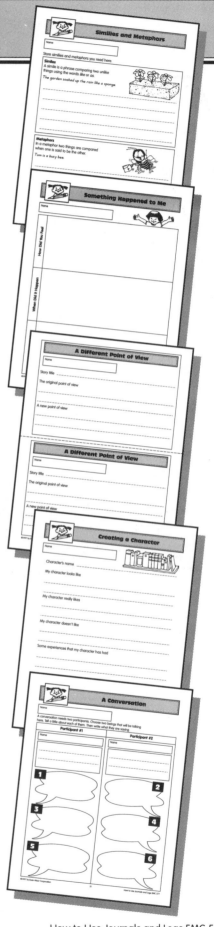

Page 27 - Special Comparisons — Similes and Metaphors

Help your students to look for similes and metaphors in their reading and they will begin to use them in their writing. Encourage them to make these special comparisons. This page provides a spot to store comparisons that your students like. As they write, they can refer back to this list for ideas.

Page 28 - Something Happened to Me

The best writing often comes from personal experiences. Encourage your students to record interesting things that have happened to them on this log page. Everyday happenings become interesting stories when revisited and developed.

Page 29 - A Different Point of View

Help your students to recognize the point of view from which a story is told. This page provides a space to practice retelling a story from a different point of view. The notes they make here may lead to a story. For example, the traditional story of "The Three Little Pigs" is told by a third person observer who sympathizes with the pigs. In Jon Scieszka's "The True Story of the 3 Little Pigs" (Viking, 1989), the story becomes very different when told from the wolf's point of view. Similarly, an account of arriving late to school may be different when told from your student's point of view and a parent's point of view.

Page 30 - Creating a Character

Developing a character before writing begins helps the author to know how the character would react and what kinds of things the character would do. Knowing a character means that an author can plan character changes that will occur and make them realistic. Use this Creating a Character page to help your students know their characters before they write about them.

Page 31 - A Conversation

This journal page provides the format for transcribing a conversation. It might be a real or an imagined conversation. The beginning could easily be developed into a story, a persuasive essay, an editorial, or a historical sketch.

My Writer's Log

Name

Words That Make You Feel...

Name

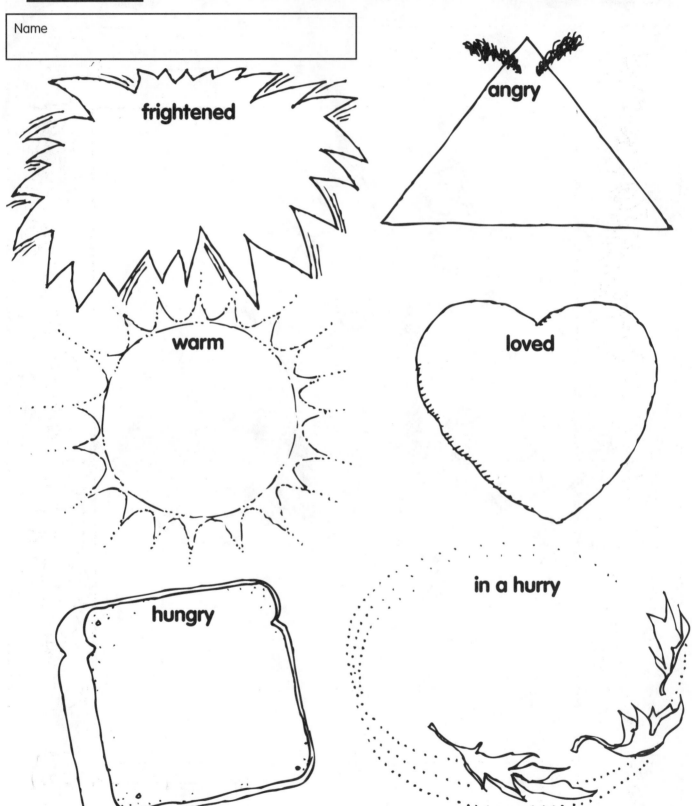

frightened

angry

warm

loved

hungry

in a hurry

24

A Frog in Her Throat
• A List of Idioms •

Name

Idiom	What it means	If I didn't know, I'd think...
a frog in her throat	She's hoarse.	

26

Similies and Metaphors

Name

Store similies and metaphors you read here.

Similes

A simile is a phrase comparing two unlike things using the words *like* or *as*.

The garden soaked up the rain like a sponge.

_____

_____

_____

_____

Metaphors

In a metaphor two things are compared when one is said to be the other.

Tom is a busy bee.

_____

_____

_____

_____

Something Happened to Me

Name

How Did You Feel	When Did it Happen	What Happened

A Different Point of View

Name _____

Story title _____

The original point of view

_____

_____

A new point of view

_____

_____

A Different Point of View

Name _____

Story title _____

The original point of view

_____

_____

A new point of view

_____

_____

Creating a Character

Name

Character's name _____

My character looks like

_____

_____

My character really likes

_____

_____

My character doesn't like

_____

_____

Some experiences that my character has had

_____

_____

_____

My character's dreams

_____

_____

A Conversation

Name

A conversation needs two participants. Choose two beings that will be talking here. Tell a little about each of them. Then write what they are saying.

Participant #1	Participant #2
Name	Name

1

2

3

4

5

6

How to Use Journals and Logs EMC 577

Learning Logs

Learning Logs are usually kept for a particular subject. For example, students might keep a science learning log or a math learning log. Pages 34-44 are reproducible forms that can be used in any subject. Reproduce them for individual students, use them to make transparencies for use with an overhead projector, or scan them to use with your computer.

Page 34 - Learning Log Cover

Page 35 - What Happened Today?

This log page is simply a form for a daily summary of what happened in a particular curriculum area, e.g. math.

- The log might be completed by a different student each day to produce a running record of what happened in class. This record is particularly valuable to those who have been absent.

- Or students might keep their own daily log of what happened making concise notations about the material and concepts covered and then noting questions that they have.

Page 36 - Passport to Success

This passport is a miniature log. It provides space for students to respond to units on different topics. For example, a study of Africa might include "stops" in six different countries so the Passport Learning Log could be used to note specific responses for each country. This mini-log can be used to record responses to any study topic with parts or distinct skills. (Fold as shown.)

Page 37 - The Important Thing List

Before students begin a reading assignment in a subject area, identify the purpose for reading, such as:

- find out the ways farmers harvest their crops
- find as many uses for water power as you can

Encourage students to read with this purpose in mind, noticing related information. When students have completed their reading, have them list in their logs everything they remember that relates to the purpose. Students then meet in groups to discuss their responses, agree on important items, and prepare The Important Thing List. The list becomes an important reference.

Page 38 - What If?

Encourage students to ask questions by including this page in their learning logs. Students ask questions about what will happen if circumstances or variables changed. Room is left to answer those "what if" questions which are not hypothetical.

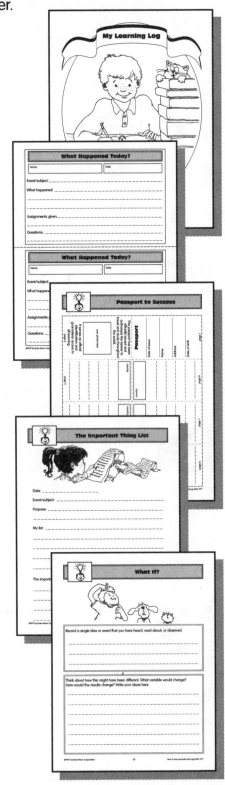

Page 39 - Making Connections

This log page format is particularly useful in history to help students make connections between the information they are learning about the past and the reality that they know.

Page 40 - K W L Chart

The K - W - L Chart is a valuable strategy for helping students connect what they already know to a new area of study.

Step 1 (K): Students list everything they **know** about a topic.
Step 2 (W): Students list what they **want** to know.
Step 3 (L): Students enter information **learned**.

Page 41 - Looking for Answers

This chart provides a format for students to use when they are looking for answers to specific questions. They begin by recording what they know and then list answers from several other sources. Then they summarize the information that they have found.

Page 42 - Making Comparisons

The Venn diagram format of this log page helps students to identify attributes that two things have in common. Label it to fit your specific needs and have students use it to record their ideas.

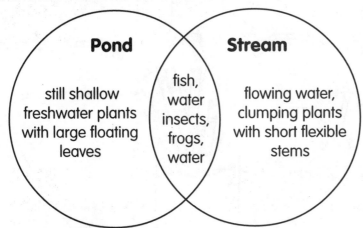

Page 43 - My Dictionary

This page provides a place for students to create their own dictionary for a specific subject or unit of study. The example can be in the form of a sentence using the word or a picture of the word. Make blank pages available so that students can add to their dictionaries at any time. Punch a hole in the corner and use a ring clip for easy addition of pages.

Page 44 - How I Did It

Use this page to help students gain proficiency in verbalizing their problem-solving strategies in math and science.

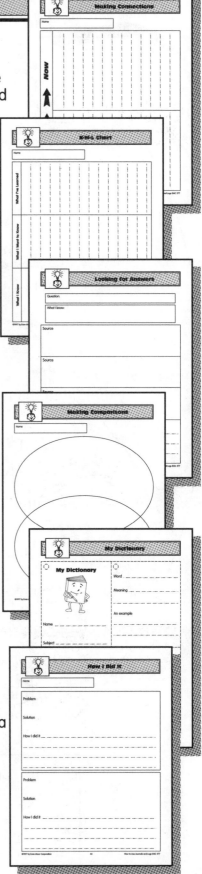

My Learning Log

Name

Subject

What Happened Today?

Name	Date

Event/subject: _____

What happened: _____

_____

_____

Assignments given: _____

_____

Questions: _____

_____

What Happened Today?

Name	Date

Event/subject: _____

What happened: _____

_____

_____

Assignments given: _____

_____

Questions: _____

_____

Passport

Date of issue _____

Name _____

Address _____

Date of birth _____

This passport has been officially issued and authorizes the bearer to travel and study throughout the world.

your photo here

It serves as official identification and guarantees access to all learning.

country

country

country

country

country

country

The Important Thing List

Date: _____

Event/subject: _____

Purpose: _____

_____

My list: _____

_____

_____

_____

_____

My group's important thing list: _____

_____

_____

_____

What If?

Record a single idea or event that you have heard, read about, or observed.

_____

_____

_____

Think about how this might have been different. What variable would change?
How would the results change? Write your ideas here.

_____

_____

_____

_____

_____

_____

Making Connections

Name

Now ↑

Then ↑

K-W-L Chart

Name

What I've Learned	What I Want to Know	What I Know

Looking for Answers

Question:

What I know:

Source

Source

Source

My summary

_____

_____

_____

Name

42

My Dictionary

( )

Name _____

Subject _____

( )

Word _____

Meaning _____

_____

An example

_____

_____

( )

Word _____

Meaning _____

_____

An example

_____

_____

( )

Word _____

Meaning _____

_____

An example

_____

_____

How I Did It

Name

Problem

Solution

How I did it _____

_____

_____

_____

Problem

Solution

How I did it _____

_____

_____

_____

Dialogue Journals

In a Dialogue Journal, students are free to write about anything they wish. What makes it a dialogue journal is that someone else, most frequently the teacher, responds to the students' entries.

You need not respond to every entry in every student's journal. Rather, address your written response to a series of entries, or one particular entry. Encourage students to tell you when they wish a response to a particular journal entry.

Many times the entries will be individualized with the topic determined by the previous response or something that is on the student's mind that day. However, it is sometimes helpful to provide prompts that will encourage responses at times when writers are "stuck."

Create a chart for your classroom using the list of prompts below or make the list into a transparency. Have the chart available so that students can refer to it as they write in their journals.

Consider writing about one of these...

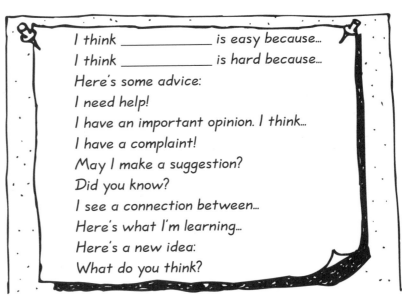

I think _____ is easy because...
I think _____ is hard because...
Here's some advice:
I need help!
I have an important opinion. I think...
I have a complaint!
May I make a suggestion?
Did you know?
I see a connection between...
Here's what I'm learning...
Here's a new idea:
What do you think?

Pages 47-50 are reproducible forms to use with your dialogue journals. Reproduce them for individual students, use them to make transparencies for use on the overhead projector, or scan them to use with your computer.

Page 47 - Full Page - Dialogue Journal Cover
Attach it to a spiral notebook for a ready-made journal.

Page 48 - Half Page - Dialogue Journal
Cover patterns for a smaller dialogue journal. Staple 5 1/2" x 8 1/2" (14 x 21.5 cm) writing paper between the covers. Cover the staples with heavy tape.

Page 49 - Dialogue with a Character

Students love carrying on a dialogue with a character in a story that they are reading. The dialogue offers them the opportunity to ask why characters did something, what characters thought about a certain event, and what they would have done if things had been different.

This project requires time to respond to the letters written by your students. You may want to enlist the help of some cross-age tutors who are familiar with the character. Encourage student helpers to carefully research the character's background so that their responses will be believable.

A postcard format may facilitate this conversation. Students write on the back of the postcard form. Collect all the postcards and hook them together with yarn or a metal ring. What fun to have a flip-book reminder of this dialogue!

Page 50 - Dialogue with a School Mascot

Emergent writers and reluctant writers enjoy writing when they know that their efforts will be rewarded with an answer. While a journal, filled with so many blank pages, may seem overwhelming to them, they will readily write an individual note.

1. If your school has a school mascot, set up a mail drop in your classroom for writing to the mascot.
2. Compose a note from the mascot asking students in your class to respond. In the note explain the procedures for sending and receiving these special messages.
3. Set out notepaper and pencils and wait.
4. **Important!** When a student writes a note, your mascot should respond the following day. Deliver the return message and help the student to read the response. This quick response encourages more writing.

Save the messages in individual student folders. Over time they will document improvement in writing skills.

Between
You and Me

Name

Note: Postcard Pattern, See Dialogue with Character on page 46.

Note: See Dialogue with a School Mascot on page 46.

Note: See Dialogue with a School Mascot on page 46.

Field Notebooks

The Field Notebook is a log that contains records of observations, reactions, and questions gathered outside of the classroom. Use the following reproducible forms and the suggestions for their use to enhance your field instruction. Create a single notebook for all your field experiences throughout the year, or make a notebook for each special occasion.

Reproduce the pages for individual students, use them to make transparencies for use with an overhead projector, or scan them for use with your computer.

Page 53 - Field Notebook Cover

Page 54 - A Survey

One way to gather data is to take a survey. Help your students to plan a survey that relates to your current area of study. The form provides space to record individuals' response to a single question. Create a graph summarizing the information gathered.

Some surveys will need to take place over a period of time. Complete the survey forms and save them in your field notebooks. Be sure to take the time to analyze the survey information and note the changes that you see occurring over time.

Page 55 - Interviews

Another way to gather data outside the classroom is to conduct interviews. Fill in the boxes on the form with questions that address the information that you hope to gain from your interviews.

Page 56 - Front Page News

Collect news that can be used in a classroom newspaper. Give each "reporter" in your classroom a mini-news pad and encourage them to keep their eyes and ears open.

Have them
- conduct interviews
- report on special occasions
- write editorials

Page 57 - Helping Your World

Ask your students to be on the lookout for examples of things individuals can do to protect the environment. They should record what they notice on their Helping Our World record page. As the lists get longer, consider writing a class environmental action handbook. Emphasize actions that are "real" for your students. Begin with your own classroom practices.

Page 58 - Growth Charts

Measuring change is important to documenting change. This notebook page can be used to record measurements for a short term project or to record measurements taken over an entire year. Keeping the data in one place and always including the same information is important to drawing final conclusions.

Page 59-64 - Field Trip Journal

Prepare a special journal to take along on field trips. For younger students, prepare one journal for the adult supervisor of each group. For older students, assign one recorder for each group and make that student responsible for the journal. Each journal should contain:

- a list of group members
- expectations for behavior
- a schedule
- a map of the area or building
- suggestions for things to see
- questions or activities that will require group discussion and reaction

This special journal will require some pre-field trip work for you. Make a pre-visit to map out suggestions for special things to see and set up the time schedule. The time you spend preparing for the trip will be well-spent as your students make the best use of every minute.

For more economical reproduction, the forms on pages 59-64 are printed two-up. Cut file folders in half to make covers for the notebook. Punch a hole in the cover and attach a pen or pencil. For younger groups, fill in much of the information before reproducing. Older students can fill in group members, rules, schedule, etc., themselves.

My Field Notebook

Name

My Survey

Question:

Names	Responses

An Interview Form

Name

Person interviewed:

Question: ....

Answer: ....

....

Question: ....

Answer: ....

....

Question: ....

Answer: ....

....

Question: ....

Answer: ....

....

Note: See Front Page News on page 51.

NEWS FLASH

NAME ....

Helping Our World

Name

I've noticed these things...	I think I can...

How to Use Journals and Logs EMC 577

See How It Grows

Name

Date: _____

Measurement: _____

Comments: _____

_____

_____

See how it looks:

Date: _____

Measurement: _____

Comments: _____

_____

_____

See how it looks:

Date: _____

Measurement: _____

Comments: _____

_____

_____

See how it looks:

Name

My Field Trip Journal

Date of trip _____

Destination _____

Name

My Field Trip Journal

Date of trip _____

Destination _____

This is your group...

Leader _____

Group members _____   _____

_____   _____

_____   _____

_____   _____

_____   _____

This is your group...

Leader _____

Group members _____   _____

_____   _____

_____   _____

_____   _____

_____   _____

Expectations for Behavior

1. _____

2. _____

3. _____

4. _____

Expectations for Behavior

1. _____

2. _____

3. _____

4. _____

Schedule

Method of transportation_____

We are leaving school at: _____

Trip schedule: _____

_____

_____

_____

We arrive back at school at: _____

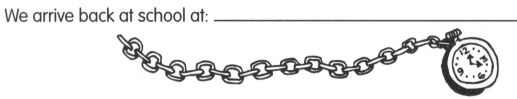

Schedule

Method of transportation_____

We are leaving school at: _____

Trip schedule: _____

_____

_____

_____

We arrive back at school at: _____

Map of Field Trip Destination and/or Route

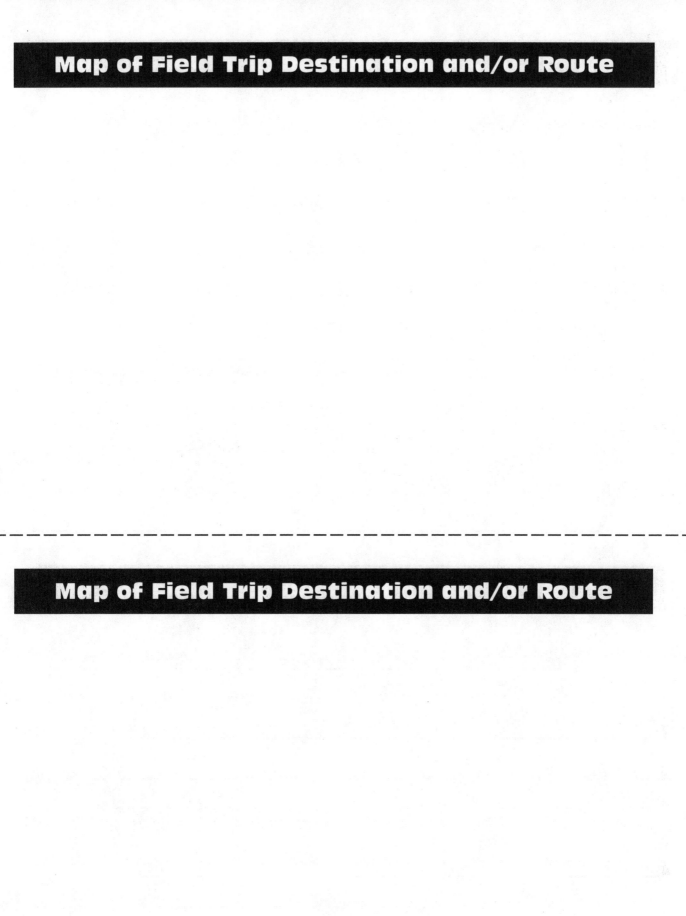

Map of Field Trip Destination and/or Route

Things to See and Questions to Answer

1. ....

2. ....

3. ....

4. ....

5. ....

Things to See and Questions to Answer

1. ....

2. ....

3. ....

4. ....

5. ....